# THE WISDOM OF JFK

# THE
# WISDOM
# OF
# JFK

Edited by T. S. SETTEL

1965

NEW YORK ‡ E. P. DUTTON & CO., INC.

# PREFACE

"John Fitzgerald Kennedy," said Cardinal Cushing of Boston, "became the voice of mankind to interpret the issues of the day and to help our generation to higher levels toward an era of relaxing tensions, humane hopes and peace on earth." Adlai Stevenson, describing Kennedy's wisdom, rhetoric and his ability to move his audiences, referred to two famous classical orators and observed, "When Cicero finished an oration, the people would say, 'How well he spoke.' Ah, but when Demosthenes finished speaking, the people would say, 'let us march.' "

Thus did the youthful President impress the world with an ageless wisdom and the rhetoric of a man far beyond his years. The many tributes to Kennedy's sensitive and critical mind bear witness to the fact that the brilliance of his words has caught the imagination of the civilized world.

John Fitzgerald Kennedy had a rare capacity to express himself, clearly interpreting the problems of the nation and the world.

During his short three years of office, President Kennedy made a great number of speeches, wrote innumerable letters and official messages, wrote thousands of words for public delivery. His wisdom and eloquence will undoubtedly rank with that of Jefferson, Lincoln, Wilson and Roosevelt, men whom Kennedy himself enjoyed quoting. Future generations will surely be quoting our late President. In this small selection of the wisdom of JFK will be found some of the words most likely to make their mark in history.

*T. S. Settel*

# CONTENTS

# CONTENTS

# Part I

NATIONAL PURPOSE
SOCIAL WELFARE
CIVIL RIGHTS
YOUTH AND EDUCATION
CULTURE AND THE ARTS
SCIENCE
CONSERVATION
EXPLORATION OF THE SEA

# Part I

# NATIONAL PURPOSE

. . . ask not what your country can do for you—ask what you can do for your country.

My fellow citizens of the world: ask not what America will do for you, but what together we can do for the freedom of man.

Finally, whether you are citizens of America or citizens of the world, ask of us here the same high standards of strength and sacrifice which we ask of you. With a good conscience our only sure reward, with history the final judge of our deeds, let us go forth to lead the land we love, asking His blessing and His help, but knowing that here on earth God's work must truly be our own.

. . . . .

Let the word go forth from this time and place, to friend and foe alike, that the torch has been passed to a new generation of Americans—born in this century, tempered by war, disciplined by a hard and bitter peace, proud of our ancient heritage—and unwilling to witness or permit the slow undoing of those human rights to which this nation has always been committed, and to which we are committed today at home and around the world.

. . . . .

I do not believe that any of us would exchange places with any other people of any other generation. The energy, the faith, the devotion which we bring to this

endeavor will light our country and all who serve it—
and the glow from that fire can truly light the world.

*Inaugural Address, January 20, 1961*

‡           ‡

We have dared to label the Sixties the Decade of Development. But it is not the eloquence of our slogans, but
the quality of our endurance, which will determine
whether this generation of Americans deserves the leadership which history has thrust upon us.

*Message to the Congress, March 22, 1961*

‡           ‡

This country has always served as a lantern in the dark
for those who love freedom but are persecuted, in misery,
or in need. We must and will continue to show the friend-
ship of the United States by doing our share in the com-
passionate task of helping those who are refugees today
as were so many of our forefathers in the years past.

*Letter to the President of the Senate and to the Speaker
of the House proposing reorganization and reenact-
ment of refugee aid legislation, July 21, 1961*

‡　　　‡

We in the United States have found our way as a free people because we have gathered in our own traditions the experience of many peoples and lives. We have learned that tolerance and cooperation are the ways to true national strength.

*Excerpt from a statement on the Jewish High Holy Days, September 6, 1961*

‡　　　‡

Let our patriotism be reflected in the creation of confidence in one another, rather than in crusades of suspicion. Let us prove we think our country great, by striving to make it greater. And, above all, let us remember, however serious the outlook, however harsh the task, the one great irreversible trend in the history of the world is on the side of liberty—and we, for all time to come, are on the same side.

*Dinner of the Democratic Party of California, November 18, 1961*

‡　　　‡

As President, my interest is in an economy which will be strong enough to absorb the potential of a rapidly expanding population, steady enough to avert the wide swings which bring grief to so many of our people, and non-inflationary enough to persuade investors that this country holds a steady promise of growth and stability.

My specific interest at this time is in maintaining a competitive world position that will not further stir the gold at Fort Knox.

*Speech before the United States Chamber of Commerce on its 50th anniversary, April 30, 1962*

‡ ‡

This Administration has sought to acknowledge our needs and look upon our obligations not by the dimming lights of the past but the rising lights of the future. We are pledged to both candor and commitment, to frank assessment and forceful action. It is in this spirit that we address ourselves to the meaning of this Labor Day. . . . that having done well, we will strive to do better; having achieved much, we determine to achieve more; having received freedom, we propose to enlarge it; having been granted the great gift of citizenship in these United States, we will reciprocate in the only coin that free men consider equal to their worth, that of their honor and their conscience.

*Labor Day speech, September 3, 1962*

Americans have always believed in progress—Americans have always kept their eyes fixed on far horizons and new frontiers. If we are faithful to our past, we cannot be fearful of our future.

*Prepared for but deleted from the text of a speech given at Wheeling Stadium, Wheeling, West Virginia, September 27, 1962*

‡        ‡

. . . we cannot protect our economy by stagnating behind tariff walls, but the best protection possible is a mutual lowering of tariff barriers among friendly nations so that all may benefit from a free flow of goods.

*Remarks upon signing the Trade Expansion Act, October 11, 1962*

‡        ‡

First, we need to strengthen our Nation by investing in our youth.

Second, we need to strengthen our Nation by safeguarding its health.

Third, we need to strengthen our Nation by protecting the basic rights of its citizens.

Fourth, we need to strengthen our Nation by making the best and the most economical use of its resources and facilities.

*Annual Message to Congress, January 14, 1963*

‡          ‡

It is a proud privilege to be a citizen of the Great Republic, to hear its songs sung, to realize that we are the descendants of 40 million people who left other countries, other familiar scenes, to come here to the United States to build a new life, to make a new opportunity for themselves and their children.

*Annual meeting of the Anti-Defamation League of B'nai B'rith, January 31, 1963*

‡          ‡

The American economy finds itself today between the period of postwar readjustment, which was prolonged by the Korean conflict, and the potentially great boom of the late sixties and seventies, when a new flood of family formation will demand new housing, consumer goods, and other installations. If we merely sit by and wait for tomorrow's prosperity, it may never come. But if we do what we need to do today, we will reap tomorrow the benefits of growing production and income, and revenues in the Federal budget.

*Twentieth anniversary meeting of the Committee for Economic Development, May 9, 1963*

‡        ‡

Equality of opportunity does not mean equality of responsibility. All Americans must be responsible citizens, but some must be more responsible than others, by virtue of their public or their private position, their role in the family or community, their prospects for the future, or their legacy from the past.

. . . . .

. . . only a respect for the law makes it possible for free men to dwell together in peace and progress . . . law is the adhesive force in the cement of society, creating order out of chaos and coherence in place of anarchy.

. . . . .

Our privileges can be no greater than our obligations. The protection of our rights can endure no longer than the performance of our responsibilities. Each can be neglected only at the peril of the others.

. . . . .

. . . we can have only one form of aristocracy in this country, as Jefferson wrote long ago in rejecting John Adams' suggestion of an artificial aristocracy of wealth and birth. It is, he wrote, the natural aristocracy of character and talent, and the best form of government, he added, was that which selected these men for positions of responsibility.

. . . . .

. . . not the finest and strongest men who are crowned, but they who enter the lists—for out of these the prize men are elected. So, too, in life, of the honorable and the good, it is they who act who rightly win the prizes.

*Convocation of Vanderbilt University, May 18, 1963*

‡ ‡

. . . . .

. . . . the two political parties in our history have always been divided, as Emerson said, into the party of hope and into the party of memory.

*May 23, 1963, when New York honored his birthday*

‡    ‡

Our investment in new citizens has always been a valuable source of our strength.

*Letter to the President of the Senate and to the Speaker of the House on revision of the immigration laws, July 23, 1963*

‡    ‡

This is a time of national maturity, understanding, and willingness to face issues as they are, not as we would like them to be. It is a test of ability to be farseeing and calm, as well as resolute, to keep an eye on both our dangers and our opportunities, and not to be diverted by momentary gains, or setbacks, or pressures.

*Address at the University of North Carolina upon receiving an honorary degree, October 12, 1961*

‡    ‡

The American eagle on the Presidential seal holds in his talons both the olive branch of peace and the arrows of military might. On the ceiling in the Presidential office, constructed many years ago, that eagle is facing the arrows of war on its left. But on the newer carpet on the floor, reflecting a change initiated by President Roosevelt and implemented by President Truman immediately after the war, that eagle is now facing the olive branch of peace. And it is in that spirit, the spirit of both preparedness and peace, that this Nation today is stronger than ever before—strengthened by both the increased power of our defenses and our increased efforts for peace—strengthened by both our resolve to resist coercion and our constant search for solutions. And it is in this spirit, I can assure you, that the American eagle still faces toward the olive branch of peace. In the months and years ahead, we intend to build both kinds of strength, during times of detente as well as tension, during periods of conflict as well as cooperation—until the world we pass on to our children is truly safe for diversity and freedom and the rule of laws covers all.

*University of Maine, October 19, 1963*

‡        ‡

I look forward to a great future for America—a future in which our country will match its military strength with our moral restraint, its wealth with our wisdom, its power with our purpose.

I look forward to an America which will not be afraid of grace and beauty, which will protect the beauty of our natural environment, which will preserve the great old American houses and squares and parks of our national past and which will build handsome and balanced cities for our future.

I look forward to an America which will reward achievement in the arts as we reward achievement in business or statecraft.

I look forward to an America which will steadily raise the standards of artistic accomplishment and which will steadily enlarge cultural opportunities for all of our citizens.

And I look forward to an America which commands respect throughout the world, not only for its strength, but for its civilization as well.

And I look forward to a world which will be safe not only for democracy and diversity but also for personal distinction.

*Amherst College, October 26, 1963*

‡ ‡

I believe in an America that is on the march, an America respected by all nations, friends and foes alike, an America that is moving, doing, working, trying, a strong America in a world at peace.

· · · · ·

I believe in an America where work was available to those who were willing and able to work, where the waste of idle men and machines could be avoided and where greater economic growth could provide the new jobs and the new markets that our growing Nation needed.

. . . . .

I believe in an America where the rights that I have described are enjoyed by all regardless of their race and their creed or their national origin.

*Remarks made at a dinner sponsored by the Democratic County Executive Committee, Philadelphia, October 30, 1963*

‡ ‡

Winston Churchill once said that democracy is the worst form of government except for all the other systems that have been tried. It is the most difficult. It requires more of you—discipline, character, self-restraint, a willingness to serve the public interest as well as our private interests.

*Speech before the National Convention of the Catholic Youth Organization, November 15, 1963*

. . . . .

‡ ‡

. . . this country is moving and it must not stop. It cannot stop. For this is a time for courage and a time for challenge. Neither conformity nor complacency will do. Neither the fanatics nor the faint-hearted are needed. And our duty as a party is not to our party alone, but to the Nation, and, indeed, to all mankind. Our duty is not merely the preservation of political power but the preservation of peace and freedom.

So let us not be petty when our cause is so great. Let us not quarrel amongst ourselves when our Nation's future is at stake. Let us stand together with renewed confidence in our cause—united in our heritage of the past and our hopes for the future—and determined that this land we love shall lead all mankind into new frontiers of peace and abundance.

*Conclusion of speech prepared for the Texas Democratic State meeting in the Municipal Auditorium in Austin, Texas, November 22, 1963*

‡ ‡

In a world of complex and continuing problems, in a world full of frustrations and irritations, America's leadership must be guided by the lights of learning and reason—or else those who confuse rhetoric with reality and the plausible with the possible will gain the popular ascendancy with their seemingly swift and simple solutions to every world problem.

There will always be dissident voices heard in the land, expressing opposition without alternatives, finding fault but never favor, perceiving gloom on every side and seeking influence without responsibility.

*From speech scheduled to be made at the Trade Mart in Dallas, November 22, 1963, but never made because of the President's death*

‡       ‡

Around the world, cracks in the monolithic apparatus of our adversary are there for all to see. This, for the American people, is a time for vision, for patience, for work and for wisdom. For better or worse, we are the pacesetters. Freedom's leader cannot flag or falter, or another runner will set the pace.

*Special message to the Congress on free-world defense assistance programs, April 2, 1963*

‡       ‡

# SOCIAL WELFARE

Now the trumpet summons us again—not as a call to bear arms, though arms we need—not as a call to battle, though embattled we are—but a call to bear the burden of a long twilight struggle year in and year out, "rejoicing in hope, patient in tribulation"—a struggle against the common enemies of man: tyranny, poverty, disease and war itself.

*Inaugural Address, January 20, 1961*

‡　　　‡

The health of our nation is a key to its future—to its economic vitality, to the morale and efficiency of its citizens, to our success in achieving our own goals and demonstrating to others the benefits of a free society.

· · · · ·

The health of the American people must ever be safeguarded; it must ever be improved. As long as people are stricken by a disease which we have the ability to prevent, as long as people are chained by a disability which can be reversed, as long as needless death takes its toll, then American health will be unfinished business.

*Special message to the Congress on health and hospital care, February 9, 1961*

‡        ‡

A nation that is partly ill-housed is not as strong as a nation with adequate homes for every family. A nation with ugly, crime-infested cities and haphazard suburbs does not present the same image to the world as a nation characterized by bright and orderly urban development.

*Special message to the Congress on housing and community development, March 9, 1961*

‡        ‡

We must resume with full vigor the forward movement toward a better life for all Americans. Essential to such a better life is housing available to all at a cost all can afford. And just as important, to the increasing number of us who choose to live in and near cities, is an orderly and healthy urban environment.

*Letter to the President of the Senate and to the Speaker of the House transmitting a Housing and Urban Improvement Bill, March 29, 1961*

✠          ✠

The basic resource of a nation is its people. Its strength can be no greater than the health and vitality of its population. Preventable sickness, disability and physical or mental incapacity are matters of both individual and national concern.

. . . . .

Good health is a prerequisite to the enjoyment of "pursuit of happiness." Whenever the miracles of modern medicine are beyond the reach of any group of Americans, for whatever reason—economic, geographic, occupational or other—we must find a way to meet their needs and fulfill their hopes. For one true measure of a nation is its success in fulfilling the promise of a better life for each of its members. Let this be the measure of our nation.

*Special message to the Congress on national health needs, February 27, 1962*

✠          ✠

Our national record in providing for our aged is a proud and hopeful one. But it can and must improve. We can continue to move forward—by building needed

Federal programs—by developing means for comprehensive action in our communities—and by doing all we can, as a nation and as individuals, to enable our senior citizens to achieve both a better standard of life and a more active, useful and meaningful role in a society that owes them much and can still learn much from them.

· · · · ·

This increase in the life span and in the number of our senior citizens presents this Nation with increased opportunities: the opportunity to draw upon their skill and sagacity—and the opportunity to provide the respect and recognition they have earned. It is not enough for a great Nation merely to have added new years to life—our objective must also be to add new life to those years.

· · · · ·

In the last three decades, this Nation has made considerable progress in assuring our older citizens the security and dignity a lifetime of labor deserves. But "the last of life, for which the first was made . . ." is still not a "golden age" for all our citizens. Too often, these years are filled with anxiety, illness, and even want. The basic statistics on income, housing and health are both revealing and disturbing.

*Special message to the Congress on the needs of the Nation's senior citizens, February 21, 1963*

‡           ‡

It was said, in an earlier age, that the mind of a man is a far country which can neither be approached nor explored. But, today, under present conditions of scientific achievement, it will be possible for a nation as rich in human and material resources as ours to make the remote reaches of the mind accessible. The mentally ill and the mentally retarded need no longer be alien to our affections or beyond the help of our communities.

*Upon signing the bill for the construction of mental retardation facilities and community mental health centers, October 31, 1963*

‡      ‡

I believe that every American family should live in a decent home in a decent neighborhood.

*Remarks made at a dinner sponsored by the Democratic County Executive Committee, Philadelphia, October 30, 1963*

‡      ‡

My fellow citizens, this is a matter which affects our country and its future. We are talking about more jobs; we are talking about the future of our country, about its strength and growth and stability as the leader of the free world. We are talking about helping people, people who have been looking for work for a long time in Eastern Kentucky, in West Virginia and Pennsylvania, the steel towns of Ohio, Gary, Indiana, Southern Illinois, other parts of our country, some of our mill towns; we are talking about a tax cut in the pockets of our people that will help create jobs and income for everyone.

We are talking . . . about one of the most important pieces of legislation to come before the Congress in 15 years. That bill could be weakened or deferred. It could be put off for another year. It could be cut down. It needs your support. This is not a question of party. It is a question of the growth of our country, of the jobs and security of our people. It is a question of whether our taxpayers and businessmen and workers will get the help they deserve.

*Radio and television address to the Nation on the Nuclear Test Ban Treaty and the Tax Reduction Bill, September 18, 1963*

‡        ‡

# CIVIL RIGHTS

*As a Senator, Kennedy spoke before a group of Democrats and Republicans in Jackson, Mississippi, just after the Supreme Court decision against segregation. His Democratic colleagues in Washington had advised him not to appear. The State Republican Chairman challenged the young Senator to give his views on segregation. Kennedy said:*

I have no hesitancy in telling the State Republican Chairman the same thing I have said in my own city of Boston, that I accept the Supreme Court decision as the supreme law of the land. I think most of us agree on the necessity to uphold law and order.

*There was silence in the room. Senator Kennedy continued:*

And now I challenge the Republican Chairman to tell us where *he* stands on Eisenhower and Nixon.

‡        ‡

The distance we have traveled in eliminating prejudice is a measure of the distance we still must travel.

*Labor Day, September 3, 1962*

. . . our nation is founded on the principle that observance of the law is the eternal safeguard of liberty, and defiance of the law is the surest road to tyranny. The law which we obey includes the final rulings of the courts, as well as the enactments of our legislative bodies. Even among law abiding men, few laws are universally loved but they are uniformly respected and not resisted.

. . . . .

Americans are free to disagree with the law but not to disobey it. For in a government of laws and not of men, no man, however prominent or powerful, and no mob, however unruly or boisterous, is entitled to defy a court of law. If this country should ever reach the point where any man or group of men, by force or threat of force, could long defy the commands of our court and our Constitution, then no law would stand free from doubt, no judge would be sure of his writ, and no citizen would be safe from his neighbors.

*Speech to the Nation at the time of the Mississippi violence in September, 1962*

‡          ‡

We preach freedom around the world, and we mean it, and we cherish our freedom here at home. But are we to say to the world, and much more importantly to each other, that this is a land of the free except for the Negroes; that we have no class or caste system, no ghettoes, no master race except with respect to Negroes?

We have a right to expect that the Negro community will be responsible, will uphold the law, but they have a right to expect that the law will be fair, that the Constitution will be color blind, as Justice Harlan said at the turn of the century.

*Radio and television report to the American people on civil rights, June 11, 1963*

‡        ‡

The centennial of the issuance of the Emancipation Proclamation is an occasion for celebration, for a sober assessment of our failures, and for rededication to the goals of freedom. Surely there could be no more meaningful observance of the centennial than the enactment of effective civil rights legislation and the continuation of effective executive action.

*Special message to the Congress on civil rights, February 28, 1963*

‡        ‡

"In giving freedom to the slaves," President Lincoln said, "we assure freedom to the free." In giving rights to others which belong to them, we give rights to ourselves and to our country.

*Remarks recorded for the ceremony at the Lincoln Memorial commemorating the centennial of the Emancipation Proclamation, September 22, 1962*

‡          ‡

We cannot afford to be complacent while any individual's rights are denied or abused.

*Letter to the Chairman in response to a report on Mississippi by the Civil Rights Commission, April 19, 1963*

‡          ‡

Justice cannot wait for too many meetings. It cannot wait for the action of the Congress or the courts. We face a moment of moral and constitutional crisis, and men of generosity and vision must make themselves heard in every section of this country. I do not say that all men are equal in their ability, their character, or their motivation, but I say they should be equal in their chance to develop their character, their motivation, and their ability. They should be given a fair chance to develop all the talents that they have, which is a basic assumption and presumption of this democracy of ours.

*Address at the United States conference of mayors in Honolulu, June 8, 1963*

‡          ‡

One hundred years of delay have passed since President Lincoln freed the slaves, yet their heirs, their grandsons, are not fully free. They are not yet freed from the bonds of injustice. They are not yet freed from social and economic oppression. And this Nation, for all its hopes and all its boasts, will not be fully free until all its citizens are free.

• • • • •

It ought to be possible, for every American to enjoy the privileges of being American without regard to his race or his color. In short, every American ought to have the right to be treated as he would wish to be treated, as one would wish his children to be treated.

*Radio and television report to the American people on civil rights, June 11, 1963*

‡        ‡

I ask you to look into your hearts—not in search of
charity, for the Negro neither wants nor needs conde-
scension—but for the one plain, proud, and priceless
quality that unites us all as Americans: a sense of justice.
In this year of the Emancipation Centennial, justice requires us to insure the blessings of liberty for all Americans and their posterity—not merely for reasons of
economic efficiency, world diplomacy, and domestic
tranquility—but, above all, because it is right.

*From a special message to the Congress on civil rights
and job opportunities, June 19, 1963*

‡        ‡

# YOUTH AND EDUCATION

Our progress as a nation can be no swifter than our progress in education. Our requirements for world leadership, our hopes for economic growth and the demands of citizenship itself in an era such as this all require the maximum development of every young American's capacity.

$$\cdot \ \cdot \ \cdot \ \cdot \ \cdot$$

Our twin goals must be: a new standard of excellence in education—and the availability of such excellence to all who are willing and able to pursue it.

$$\cdot \ \cdot \ \cdot \ \cdot \ \cdot$$

The human mind is our fundamental resource. A balanced Federal program must go well beyond incentives for investment in plant and equipment. It must include equally determined measures to invest in human beings —both in their basic education and training and in their more advanced preparation for professional work. Without such measures, the Federal Government will not be carrying out its responsibilities for expanding the base of our economic and military strength.

$$\cdot \ \cdot \ \cdot \ \cdot \ \cdot$$

We do not undertake to meet our growing educational problems merely to compare our achievements with those of our adversaries. These measures are justified on their own merits—in times of peace as well as peril, to educate better citizens as well as better scientists and soldiers. The Federal Government's responsibility in this area has

been established since the earliest days of the Republic—
it is time now to act decisively to fulfill that responsibility
for the sixties.

*Special message to the Congress on education,*
*February 20, 1961*

‡          ‡

Young Americans must be made fit—to serve our nation in its hour of need—fit to face the future with confidence and strength.

*Statement by the President on the physical fitness of*
*young Americans, September 5, 1961*

‡          ‡

We do not want in the United States a nation of spec-
tators. We want a nation of participants in the vigorous
life.

*Speech to the Youth Fitness Conference,*
*February 21, 1961*

‡          ‡

The Greeks sought excellence not only in philosophy and drama and sculpture and architecture, but in athletics. The same people who produced the poetry of Homer, the wisdom of Plato and Aristotle—they also produced the Olympic Games. The Greeks understood that mind and body must develop in harmonious proportion to produce a creative intelligence. And so did the most brilliant intelligence of our earliest days, Thomas Jefferson, when he said, "Not less than two hours a day should be devoted to exercise." If a man who wrote the Declaration of Independence, was Secretary of State, and twice President could give it two hours, our children can give it 10 or 15 minutes.

. . . . .

We are under-exercised as a nation. We look, instead of play. We ride, instead of walk. Our existence deprives us of the minimum of physical activity essential for healthy living, and the remedy, in my judgment, lies in one direction; that is, in developing programs for broad participation in exercise by all of our young men and women—all of our boys and girls.

*Address to the National Football Foundation and Hall of Fame Banquet, New York City, December 5, 1961*

‡ ‡

. . . education is both the foundation and the unifying force of our democratic way of life—it is the mainspring of our economic and social progress—it is the highest expression of achievement in our society, ennobling and enriching human life. In short, it is at the same time the most profitable investment society can make and the richest reward it can confer.

. . . . .

The education of our people is a national investment. It yields tangible returns in economic growth, an improved citizenry and higher standards of living. But even more importantly, free men and women value education as a personal experience and opportunity—as a basic benefit of a free and democratic civilization. It is our responsibility to do whatever needs to be done to make this opportunity available to all and to make it of the highest possible quality.

*Special message to the Congress on education,*
*February 6, 1962*

‡          ‡

. . . knowledge, not hate, is the passkey to the future —that knowledge transcends national antagonisms—that it speaks a universal language—that it is the possession, not of a single class, or of a single nation or a single ideology, but of all mankind.

*University of California, Berkeley, March 23, 1962*

‡          ‡

Education is the keystone in the arch of freedom and progress. . . .

For the individual, the doors to the schoolhouse, to the library and to the college lead to the richest treasures of our open society: to the power of knowledge—to the training and skills necessary for productive employment —to the wisdom, the ideals, and the culture which enrich life—and to the creative, self-disciplined understanding of society needed for good citizenship in today's changing and challenging world.

. . . . .

For the Nation, increasing the quality and availability of education is vital to both our national security and our domestic well-being. A free Nation can rise no higher than the standard of excellence set in its schools and colleges.

*Special message to the Congress on education, January 29, 1963*

‡          ‡

A common subject of discussion in mid-century America is assigning the blame for our mounting juvenile delinquency—to parents, schools, courts, communities and others, including the children themselves. There is no single answer—and no single cause or cure. But surely the place to begin is the malady which underlies so much of youthful frustration, rebellion and idleness: and that malady is a lack of opportunity.

This lack cannot be cured without a more perfect educational and vocational training system, a more prosperous full employment economy, the removal of racial barriers, and the elimination of slum housing and dilapidated neighborhoods.

．．．．．

The most direct, rewarding and important investment in our children and youth is education. A high rate of investment in education is essential for our national economic growth, our scientific advancement and our national security. Maintaining the broadest possible opportunities in education is essential to the maintenance of democratic government and to the attainment of our social, cultural and economic aspirations.

．．．．．

. . . good physical fitness is essential to good physical and mental health. If our young men and women are to attain the social, scientific and economic goals of which they are capable, they must all possess the strength, the energy and the good health to pursue them vigorously.

．．．．．

Chronic world tensions have tended to distract our attention from those problems which have long-range rather than immediate consequences. But each passing month makes it clearer that our past failures to identify, understand and meet the many problems relating to our Nation's youth cannot be countenanced any longer. Awareness is a large part of the battle. But it is action that will spell the difference.

*Message to the Congress on the Nation's youth, February 14, 1963*

‡　　　　‡

"It is not learning," said President Wilson, "but the spirit of service that will give a college place in the public annals of the Nation." "It is indispensable," he said, "if it is to do its right service, that the air of affairs should be admitted to all its classrooms . . . the air of the world's transactions, the consciousness of the solidarity of the race, the sense of the duty of man toward man . . . the promise and the hope that shine in the face of all knowledge. . . . The days of glad expansion are gone, our life grows tense and difficult; our resource for the future lies in careful thought, providence, and a wise economy; and the school must be of the Nation."

*Address at the Boston College centennial ceremonies, April 20, 1963*

‡　　　　‡

The educated citizen has a special obligation to encourage the pursuit of learning, to promote exploration of the unknown, to preserve the freedom of inquiry, to support the advancement of research, and to assist at every level of government the improvement of education for all Americans, from grade school to graduate school.

. . . . .

. . . the educated citizen has an obligation to serve the public . . . he must be a participant and not a spectator.

. . . . .

"Every man, every man sent out from a university," said Professor Woodrow Wilson, "should be a man of his Nation, as well as a man of his time."

. . . . .

Only an educated and informed people will be a free people, that the ignorance of one voter in a democracy impairs the security of all, and that if we can, as Jefferson put it, "enlighten the people generally . . . tyranny and the oppressions of mind and body will vanish, like evil spirits at the dawn of the day."

. . . . .

. . . everything changes but change itself. We live in an age of movement and change, both evolutionary and revolutionary, both good and evil—and in such an age a university has a special obligation to hold fast to the best of the past and move fast to the best of the future.

. . . . .

. . . there will always be those who scoff at intellectuals, who cry out against research, who seek to limit our educational system. Modern cynics and skeptics see no more reason for landing a man on the moon, which we shall do, than the cynics and skeptics of half a millennium ago saw for the discovery of this country. They see no harm in paying those to whom they entrust the minds of their children a smaller wage than is paid to those to whom they entrust the care of their plumbing.

. . . . .

. . . liberty without learning is always in peril, and learning without liberty is always in vain.

*Convocation of Vanderbilt University, May 18, 1963*

‡                    ‡

The men who create power make an indispensable contribution to the nation's greatness, but the men who question power make a contribution just as indispensable, especially when that questioning is disinterested.

For they determine whether we use power or power uses us.

*Amherst College, October 26, 1963*

‡            ‡

I believe in an America which provided the maximum amount of education to the maximum number of our children, an America no longer denying a college education to one-third of our brightest students. This also is a continuing battle, and until the Congress has helped make it possible for every child of every State and station to attend a well-equipped school under well-trained and well-paid teachers, that battle must go on.

*Speech before the Democratic County Executive Committee, Philadelphia, October 30, 1963*

‡            ‡

# CULTURE AND THE ARTS

We are, even though we hesitate to admit it, a cultured people and I hope we will be more so.

When we use that word, we use it in the sense—really in the Greek sense—of the full man and woman living in a full system of freedom who develops his own resources and talents and in so doing serves the greater good of all of our people.

*White House Musical Program for Youth,*
*April 22, 1963*

‡        ‡

. . . art and the encouragement of art is political in the most profound sense, not as a weapon in the struggle, but as an instrument of understanding of the futility of struggle between those who share man's faith.

•  •  •  •  •

. . . as a great democratic society, we have a special responsibility to the arts, for art is the great democrat calling forth creative genius from every sector of society, disregarding race or religion or wealth or color. The mere accumulation of wealth and power is available to the dictator and the democrat alike.

. . . . .

. . . today, as always, art knows no national boundaries.

Genius can speak at any time, and the entire world will hear it and listen. Behind the storm of daily conflict and crisis, the dramatic confrontations, the tumult of political struggle, the poet, the artist, the musician, continues the quiet work of centuries, building bridges of experience between peoples, reminding man of the universality of his feelings and desires and despairs, and reminding him that the forces that unite are deeper than those that divide.

*Closed-circuit television broadcast on behalf of the National Cultural Center, November 29, 1962*

‡ ‡

When power leads man toward arrogance, poetry reminds him of his limitations. When power narrows the areas of man's concern, poetry reminds him of the richness and diversity of his existence. When power corrupts, poetry cleanses. For art establishes the basic human truths which must serve as the touchstones of our judgment. The artist . . . becomes the last champion of the individual mind and sensibility against an intrusive society

and an officious state. . . . I see little of more importance to the future of our country and our civilization
than full recognition of the place of the artist. If art is to
nourish the roots of our culture, society must set the
artist free to follow his vision wherever it takes him.

*Amherst College, October 26, 1963*

‡          ‡

# SCIENCE

The genius of our scientists has given us the tools to bring abundance to our land, strength to our industry, and knowledge to our people. For the first time we have the capacity to strike off the remaining bonds of poverty and ignorance—to free our people for the spiritual and intellectual fulfillment which has always been the goal of our civilization.

*White House reception for members of the Congress and the Diplomatic Corps of the Latin American republics, March 13, 1961*

‡        ‡

I would mention a problem which I know has greatly concerned many of you. That is our responsibility to control the effects of our own scientific experiments. For as science investigates the natural environment, it also modifies it, and that modification may have incalculable consequences for evil as well as for good.

*Address at the Anniversary Convocation of the National Academy of Sciences, October 22, 1963*

‡        ‡

We are bound to grope for a time as we grapple with problems without precedent in human history. But wisdom is the child of experience. In the years since man unlocked the power stored within the atom, the world has made progress, halting but effective, towards bringing that power under human control. The challenge, in short, may be our salvation. As we begin to master the destructive potentialities of modern science we move toward a new era in which science can fulfill its creative promise.

*Letter to the President of the Senate on increasing the national effort in oceanography, March 29, 1961*

‡          ‡

Science remains universal, and the fruits of science, if wisely chosen, provide a means by which humanity can realize a full and abundant life. Yet the vitality of science, its ability to enrich our culture and our understanding, and the material benefits it promises all depend in large measure upon international pooling of knowledge and effort.

*Message to the Conference on Science and World Affairs at Stowe, Vermont, September 4, 1961*

‡          ‡

If scientific discovery has not been an unalloyed blessing, if it has conferred on mankind the power not only to create, but to annihilate, it has at the same time provided humanity with a supreme challenge and a supreme testing. If the challenge and the testing are too much for humanity, then we are all doomed. But I believe that the future can be bright, and I believe it can be certain. Man is still the master of his own fate, and I believe that the power of science and the responsibility of science have offered mankind a new opportunity not only for intellectual growth, but for moral discipline; not only for the acquisition of knowledge, but for the strengthening of our nerve and our will.

*Address at the Anniversary Convocation of the National Academy of Sciences, October 22, 1963*

‡        ‡

We have left behind prejudice, superstition and ignorance which since the dawn of time distorted our thinking about the mentally retarded. We have entered a new era of understanding, hope and enlightenment. We are on the threshold of an exciting and great achievement which is a tribute to the skills and devotions of thousands of dedicated scientists, professional persons, and public and private citizens.

The transformation of the lives of millions of Americans will be realized to a very large extent through the efforts of the delegates and participants at this Conference. The retarded child will emerge from the attic of society to take his place on the school playground; and the retarded adult will move from a back bedroom or institutional ward to the day center and workshop.

There can be no greater evidence of American vitality, intelligence and humanitarian tradition.

*Letter to Dr. Stafford L. Warren at the opening of the White House Conference on Mental Retardation, September 19, 1963*

‡            ‡

Today we stand on the threshold of major discoveries in the life sciences. Albert Einstein once said that it would be a great cause of regret and would put all mankind into jeopardy if the life sciences did not keep up with the tremendous advances of the physical sciences. This is nowhere more apparent than in the field of mental retardation.

We have conquered the atom, but we have not yet begun to make a major assault upon the mysteries of the human mind. In spite of the dramatic discoveries in medicine, the number of mentally retarded is increasing. Whooping cough, diphtheria, scarlet fever, have all but been eliminated, but every year 126,000 children are born who are or who will become retarded. Parents frequently must face decisions in hospitals of what therapy should be adopted to preserve a child's life, knowing that that therapy may bring about mental retardation or blindness. Almost 5,000 of these children are so severely retarded that they will never be able to care for their own needs. This tragic human waste which of course, affects not only the child but the family which is involved, can and must be stopped.

I think we have an obligation of country, especially a country as rich as ours, especially a country which has so much money to spend on so many things which may be desirable, but may be not essential in every case—we certainly should have the resources to spend to make a major effort to see if we can block this, stop it, cure it.

*Remarks at the 13th annual convention of the National Association for Retarded Children, October 24, 1963*

‡        ‡

Frank O'Connor, the Irish writer, tells in one of his books how as a boy, he and his friends would make their way across the countryside and when they came to an orchard wall that seemed too high and too doubtful to try and too difficult to permit their voyage to continue, they took off their hats and tossed them over the wall— and then they had no choice but to follow them.

This Nation has tossed its cap over the wall of space, and we have no choice but to follow it. Whatever the difficulties, they will be overcome. Whatever the hazards, they must be guarded against. . . . with the help and support of all Americans, we will climb this wall with safety and with speed—and we shall then explore the wonders on the other side.

*Dedication of the Aerospace Medical Health Center, San Antonio, November 21, 1963*

‡     ‡

# CONSERVATION

At the inauguration, Robert Frost read a poem which began "the land was ours before we were the land's"— meaning, in part, that this new land of ours sustained us before we were a nation. And although we are now the land's—a nation of people matched to a continent—we still draw our strength and sustenance . . . from the earth.

. . . . .

. . . it is our task in our time and in our generation, to hand, down undiminished to those who come after us, as was handed down to us by those who went before, the natural wealth and beauty which is ours. To do this will require constant attention and vigilance—sustained vigor and imagination.

. . . . .

Throughout our history our soil and water, our forests and minerals, have provided the resources upon which this country grew—and our power ascended. Today, this great gift of material wealth provides the foundation upon which the defense of freedom rests, here and around the world. And our future greatness and our strength depend upon the continued abundant use of our natural resources.

*Dedication of the National Wildlife Federation Building, March 3, 1961*

‡      ‡

. . . in the field of conservation, every day that is lost is a valuable opportunity wasted. Everytime, particularly in the East where they have such a massive concentration of population—every time an acre of land disappears into private development or exploitation, an acre of land which could be used for the people, we have lost a chance. We will never get it back.

. . . . .

Theodore Roosevelt once said that the White House is a great pulpit from which to preach, and I would like to preach not only the vigorous life which he preached for us physically, but also for us in our time, facing entirely different problems, to make the same wise, vigorous decisions which he made for the conservation of our natural resources so that you and your children can enjoy this great and rich country. Nature has been so generous to us that we have mistreated her. Now, when our country is becoming increasingly crowded, when science and technology wastes so much of what we have, we have to realize that time is running out for us.

. . . . .

. . . we are the heirs of Theodore Roosevelt, and what we must do today is prepare for those who are our heirs. The steps we take in conservation and reclamation will have very little effect upon all of us here immediately and in this decade. What we are doing in the real sense is preparing for those who come after us.

*Address to the students at the University of North Dakota, September 25, 1963*

‡        ‡

There are two points on conservation that have come home to me in the last two days. One is the necessity for us to protect what we already have, what nature gave to us, and use it well, not to waste water or land, to set aside land and water, recreation, wilderness, and all the rest now so that it will be available to those who come in the future. That is the traditional concept of conservation, and it still has a major part in the national life of the United States. But the other part of conservation is the newer part, and that is to use science and technology to achieve significant breakthroughs as we are doing today, and in that way to conserve the resources which ten or twenty or thirty years ago may have been wholly unknown. So we use nuclear power for peaceful purposes and power. We use new techniques to develop new kinds of coal and oil from shale, and all the rest. We use new techniques that Senator Magnuson has pioneered in oceanography, so from the bottom of the ocean and from the ocean we get all the resources which are there, and which are going to be mined and harvested. And from the sun we are going to find more and more uses for that energy whose power we are so conscious of today.

All this means that we put science to work, science to work in improving our environment and making this country a better place in which to live.

*Speech before the Hanford, Washington, Electric Generating Plant, September 26, 1963*

‡       ‡

No water resources program is of greater long-range importance—for relief not only of our shortages, but for arid nations the world over—than our efforts to find an effective and economical way to convert water from the world's greatest, cheapest natural resources—our oceans —into water fit for consumption in the home and by industry. Such a breakthrough would end bitter struggles between neighbors, states, and nations—and bring new hope for millions who live out their lives in dire shortage of usable water and all its physical and economical blessings, though living on the edge of a great body of water throughout that parched life-time.

. . . . .

Problems of immediacy always have the advantage of attracting notice—those that lie in the future fare poorly in the competition for attention and money. . . . we cannot, however, delude ourselves—we must understand our resources problems, and we must face up to them now. The task is large but it will be done.

*Special message to the Congress on natural resources, February 23, 1961*

‡     ‡

Our goal is to investigate the world ocean, its boundaries, its properties, its processes. To a surprising extent,
the sea has remained a mystery. . . . We know less of
the oceans at our feet, where we came from, than we do
of the sky above our heads. It is time to change this, to
use to the full our powerful new instruments of oceanic
exploration, to drive back the frontiers of the unknown
in the waters which encircle our globe.

. . . . .

I can imagine no field among all those which are so
exciting today than this great effort which our country
and others will carry on in the years to come. We need
this knowledge for its own sake. We want to know what
is under the sea, and we need it to consider its bearings
on our security, and on the world's social and economic
needs. It has been estimated, for example, that the yield
of food from the seas could be increased five or ten times
through better knowledge of marine biology, and some
day we will seed and weed and harvest the ocean. Here,
again, the job can best be done by the nations of the
world working together in international institutions.

*Address at the Anniversary Convocation of the Na-
tional Academy of Sciences, October 22, 1963*

‡        ‡

The seas . . . offer a wealth of nutritional resources.
They are a principal source of protein. They can provide

many times the current food supply if we but learn how to garner and husband this self-renewing larder. To meet the vast needs of an expanding population, the bounty of the sea must be made more available. Within two decades, our own Nation will require over a million more tons of seafood than we now harvest.

. . . . .

To predict, and perhaps some day to control, changes in weather and climate is of the utmost importance to man everywhere. These changes are controlled to a large and yet unknown extent by what happens in the ocean. Ocean and atmosphere work together in a still mysterious way to determine our climate. Additional research is necessary to identify the factors in this interplay.

. . . . .

Knowledge and understanding of the oceans promise to assume greater and greater importance in the future. This is not a one year program—or even a ten-year program. It is the first step in a continuing effort to acquire and apply the information about a part of our world that will ultimately determine conditions of life in the rest of the world. The opportunities are there. A vigorous program will capture these opportunities.

*Letter to the President of the Senate on increasing the national effort in oceanography, March 29, 1961*

‡ ‡

# Part II

# PEACE

Only when our arms are sufficient beyond doubt can we be certain beyond doubt that they will never be employed.

. . . . .

. . . to those nations who would make themselves our adversary, we offer not a pledge but a request: that both sides begin anew the quest for peace, before the dark powers of destruction unleased by science engulf all humanity in planned or accidental self-destruction.

*Inaugural Address, January 20, 1961*

‡　　　‡

Where nature makes natural allies of all, we can demonstrate that beneficial relations are possible even with those with whom we most deeply disagree—and this must someday be the basis of world peace and world law.

*Annual Message to the Congress on the State of the Union, January 30, 1961*

We do not want to fight, but we have fought before. And others in earlier times have made the same dangerous mistake of assuming that the West was too selfish and too soft and too divided to resist invasions of freedom in other lands. Those who threaten to unleash the forces of war on a dispute over West Berlin should recall the words of the ancient philosopher: "A man who causes fear cannot be free from fear."

*Radio and television report to the American people on the Berlin crisis, July 25, 1961*

‡          ‡

I pledge you that we shall neither commit nor provoke aggression, that we shall neither flee nor invoke the threat of force, that we shall never negotiate out of fear, we shall never fear to negotiate.

*Address in New York City before the General Assembly of the United Nations, September 25, 1961*

‡          ‡

We must distinguish the real from the illusory, the long-range from the temporary, the significant from the petty, but if we can be purposeful, if we can face up to our risks and live up to our word, if we can do our duty undeterred by fanatics or frenzy at home or abroad, then surely peace and freedom can prevail. We shall be neither Red nor dead, but alive and free.

*Address at the University of North Carolina upon receiving an honorary degree, October 12, 1961*

‡        ‡

There is no way to maintain the frontiers of freedom without cost and commitment and risk. There is no swift and easy path to peace in our generation. No man who witnessed the tragedies of the last war, no man who can imagine the unimaginable possibilities of the next war, can advocate war out of irritability or frustration or impatience.

But let no nation confuse our perseverance and patience with fear of war or unwillingness to meet our responsibilities. We can not save ourselves by abandoning those who are associated with us, or rejecting our responsibilities.

In the end, the only way to maintain the peace is to be prepared in the final extreme to fight for our country—and to mean it.

*Veterans Day, Arlington National Cemetery, November 11, 1961*

✝        ✝

"If there is going to be trouble, let it come in my time, so that my children may live in peace."

We live in a troublesome time, but let it come in our time, so that in this country and around the world our children and their children may live in peace and security.

*President Kennedy concluded a speech in Seattle at the silver anniversary dinner honoring Senator Magnuson on November 16, 1961, with a quote from Thomas Paine*

✝        ✝

A nation which is dedicated to progress, which does not try to freeze history in its tracks, which is determined to serve the people and their welfare, and their freedom —this is the nation which is most likely to unite the people of the world against aggression and for peace.

*Remarks made by telephone to a dinner of the Ohio State Democratic Convention, Columbus, September 21, 1962*

✝        ✝

Let us preserve both the law and the peace and then healing those wounds that are within we can turn to the greater crises that are without and stand united as one people in our pledge to man's freedom.

*Radio and television report to the Nation on the situation at the University of Mississippi,*
*September 30, 1962*

‡ ‡

Neither the United States of America nor the world community of nations can tolerate deliberate deception and offensive threats on the part of any nation, large or small.

. . . . .

We no longer live in a world where only the actual firing of weapons represents a sufficient challenge to a nation's security to constitute maximum peril. Nuclear weapons are so destructive and ballistic missiles are so swift that any substantially increased possibility of their use or any sudden change in their deployment may well be regarded as a definite threat to peace.

. . . . .

We will not prematurely or unnecessarily risk the cost of worldwide nuclear war in which even the fruits of victory would be ashes in our mouth—but neither will we shrink from that risk at any time it must be faced.

. . . . .

The path we have chosen for the present is full of hazards—but it is the one most consistent with our character and courage as a nation and our commitments around the world. The cost of freedom is always high—but Americans have always paid it. And one path we shall never choose, and that is the path of surrender or submission.

Our goal is not the victory of might, but the vindication of right—not peace at the expense of freedom, but both peace and freedom, here in this hemisphere, and we hope, around the world. God willing, that goal will be achieved.

*Radio and television report to the American people on the Soviet arms buildup in Cuba, October 22, 1962*

‡          ‡

I welcome Chairman Khrushchev's statesmanlike decision to stop building bases in Cuba, to dismantle offensive weapons and return them to the Soviet Union under United Nations verification. This is an important and constructive contribution to peace . . . It is my earnest hope that the governments of the world can, with a solution of the Cuban crisis, turn their urgent attention to the necessities for ending the arms race and reducing world tensions.

*Message to the Premier of the Soviet Union, October 28, 1962*

‡                ‡

. . . in an imperfect world where human folly has
been the rule and not the exception, the surest way to
bring on the war that can never happen is to sit back and
assure ourselves it will not happen.

*Speech to the graduating class of the United States Air
Force Academy, Colorado Springs, June 5, 1963*

‡                ‡


World peace, like community peace, does not require
that each man love his neighbor—it requires only that
they live together in mutual tolerance, submitting their
disputes to a just and peaceful settlement.

.  .  .  .  .

Genuine peace must be the product of many nations,
the sum of many acts. It must be dynamic, not static,
changing to meet the challenge of each new generation.
For peace is a process—a way of solving problems.

.  .  .  .  .

Wherever we are, we must all, in our daily lives, live
up to the age-old faith that peace and freedom walk
together. In too many of our cities today, the peace is not
secure because freedom is incomplete.

"When a man's ways please the Lord," the Scriptures tell us, "he maketh even his enemies to be at peace with him." And is not peace, in the last analysis, basically a matter of human rights—the right to live out our lives without fear of devastation—the right to breathe air as nature provided it—the right of future generations to a healthy existence?

· · · · ·

We shall . . . do our part to build a world of peace where the weak are safe and the strong are just. We are not helpless before that task or hopeless of its success. Confident and unafraid, we labor on.

*Commencement address at American University, Washington, D.C., June 10, 1963*

‡       ‡

My fellow Americans, let us take that first step. Let us, if we can, step back from the shadows of war and seek out the way of peace. And if that journey is a thousand miles, or even more, let history record that we, in this land, at this time, took the first step.

*Radio and television address, July 26, 1963*

Peace is a daily, a weekly, a monthly process, gradually changing opinions, slowly eroding old barriers, quietly building new structures. And however undramatic the pursuit of peace, that pursuit must go on.

*Address before the 18th General Assembly of the United Nations, September 20, 1963*

‡ ‡

This transaction advertises to the world as nothing else could the success of free American agriculture. It demonstrates our willingness to relieve food shortages, to reduce tensions, and to improve relations with all countries. And it shows that peaceful agreements with the United States which serve the interests of both sides are a far more worthwhile course than a course of isolation and hostility.

*President's news conference, October 9, 1963, discussing the Soviet Union's willingness to buy grain from us.*

‡ ‡

Let us recognize both the gains we have made down the road to peace and the great distance yet to be covered. Let us not waste the present pause by either a needless renewal of tensions or a needless relaxation of vigilance. And let us recognize that we have made these gains and achieved this pause by the firmness we displayed a year ago as well as our restraint—by our efforts for defense as well as our efforts for peace.

. . . . .

. . . while maintaining our readiness for war, let us exhaust every avenue for peace. Let us always make clear our willingness to talk, if talk will help, and our readiness to fight, if fight we must. Let us resolve to be the masters, not the victims, of our history, controlling our own destiny without giving way to blind suspicion and emotion. Let us distinguish between our hopes and our illusions, always hoping for steady progress toward less critically dangerous relations with the Soviets, but never laboring under any illusions about Communist methods or Communist goals.

*University of Maine, October 19, 1963*

‡          ‡

Just as the Family of Man is not limited to a single race or religion, neither can it be limited to a single city or country. The Family of Man is more than three billion strong. It lives in more than 100 nations. Most of its members are not white. Most of them are not Christians. Most of them know nothing about free enterprise or due process of law or the Australian ballot.

If our society is to promote the Family of Man, let us realize the magnitude of our task. This is a sobering assignment. For the Family of Man in the world of today is not faring very well.

The members of a family should be at peace with one another, but they are not. And the hostilities are not confined to the great powers of the East and the West. On the contrary, the United States and the Soviet Union, each fully aware of their mutually destructive powers and their worldwide responsibilities and obligations, have on occasion sought to introduce a greater note of caution in their approach to areas of conflict.

Yet lasting peace between East and West would not bring peace to the Family of Man.

. . . . .

. . . even little wars are dangerous in this nuclear world. The long labor of peace is an undertaking for every nation, large and small, for every member of the Family of Man. "In this effort none of us can remain unaligned. To this goal none can be uncommitted." If the Family of Man cannot achieve greater unity and harmony, the very planet which serves as its home may find its future in peril.

*Dinner of the Protestant Council of the City of New York, November 8, 1963*

‡      ‡

We far prefer world law, in the age of self-determination, to world war, in the age of mass extermination.

· · · · ·

Together we shall save our planet, or together we shall perish in its flames. Save it we can—and save it we must —and then shall we earn the eternal thanks of mankind and, as peacemakers, the eternal blessing of God.

· · · · ·

We cannot expect that all nations will adopt like systems—for conformity is the jailer of freedom, and the enemy of growth.

· · · · ·

However difficult it may be to fill Mr. Hammarskjöld's place, it can better be filled by one man rather than by three. Even the three horses of the Troika did not have three drivers, all going in different directions. They had only one—and so must the United Nations executive. To install a triumvirate or any panel, or any rotating authority, in the United Nations administrative offices would replace order with anarchy, action with paralysis, confidence with confusion.

*Address in New York City before the General
Assembly of the United Nations, September 25, 1961*

74 ‡ THE UNITED NATIONS

The indestructible principles of the Charter exert a gravitational pull which adds strength to every aspect of our world-wide diplomacy. The United Nations, under that Charter, provides a framework within which we can pursue the highest goal of American foreign policy: a world community of independent nations living together in free association at peace with each other.

*Message to the Congress transmitting the 16th Annual Report on United States participation in the United Nations, August 2, 1962*

‡       ‡

Today the United Nations is primarily the protector of the small and the weak, and a safety valve for the strong. Tomorrow, it can form the framework for a world of law—a world in which no nation dictates the destiny of another, and in which the vast resources now devoted to destructive means will serve constructive ends.

*Annual Message to the Congress, January 14, 1963*

‡       ‡

The United Nations must be fully and fairly financed. Its peacekeeping machinery must be strengthened. Its institutions must be developed until some day, and perhaps some distant day, a world of law is achieved.

*Dublin, June 28, 1963*

‡        ‡

My fellow inhabitants of this planet: Let us take our stand here in this Assembly of nations. And let us see if we, in our own time, can move the world to a just and lasting peace.

•  •  •  •  •

The task of building the peace lies with the leaders of every nation, large and small. For the great powers have no monopoly on conflict or ambition. The cold war is not the only expression of tension in this world—and the nuclear race is not the only arms race. Even little wars are dangerous in a nuclear world. The long labor of peace is an undertaking for every nation—and in this effort none of us can remain unaligned. To this goal none can be uncommitted.

•  •  •  •  •

The effort to improve the conditions of man, however, is not a task for the few. It is the task of all nations—acting alone, acting in groups, acting in the United Nations, for plague and pestilence, and plunder and pollution, the hazards of nature, and the hunger of children are the foes of every nation. The earth, the sea, and the air are the concern of every nation. And science, technology, and education can be the ally of every nation.

Never before has man had such capacity to control his own environment, to end thirst and hunger, to conquer poverty, and disease, to banish illiteracy and massive human misery. We have the power to make this the best generation of mankind in the history of the world—or to make it the last.

. . . . .

Let us complete what we have started. For "No man who puts his hand to the plow and looks back," as the Scriptures tell us, . . . "is fit for the Kingdom of God."

. . . . .

. . . peace does not rest in charters and covenants alone. It lies in the hearts and minds of all people. And if it is cast out there, then no act, no pact, no treaty, no organization can hope to preserve it without the support and the wholehearted commitment of all people. So let us not rest all our hopes on parchment and on paper; let us strive to build for peace, in the hearts and minds of all of our people. I believe that we can. I believe the problems of human destiny are not beyond the reach of human beings.

. . . . .

New efforts are needed if this Assembly's Declaration of Human Rights, now 15 years old, is to have full meaning. And new means should be found for promoting the free expression and trade of ideas—through travel and communication, and through increased exchanges of people, and books, and broadcasts. For as the world renounces the competition of weapons, competition in ideas must flourish—and that competition must be as full and as fair as possible.

*Address before the 18th General Assembly of the United Nations, September 20, 1963*

‡　　　‡

Recent scientific advances have not only made international cooperation desirable, but they have made it essential. The ocean, the atmosphere, outer space, belong not to one nation or one ideology, but to all mankind, and as science carries out its tasks in the years ahead it must enlist all its own disciplines, all nations prepared for the scientific quest, and all men capable of sympathizing with the scientific impulse.

. . . . .

The earth can be an abundant mother to all of the people that will be born in the coming years if we learn to use her with skill and wisdom to heal her wounds, replenish her vitality, and utilize her potentialities. And the necessity is now urgent and worldwide, for few nations embarked on the adventure of development have the resources to sustain an ever-growing population and a rising standard of living. The United Nations has designated this the Decade of Development. We all stand committed to make this agreeable hope a reality. This seems to me the greatest challenge to science in our times, to use the world's resources, to expand life and hope for the world's inhabitants.

*Address at the Anniversary Convocation of the National Academy of Sciences, October 22, 1963*

‡        ‡

# DISARMAMENT AND THE
# NUCLEAR TEST BAN TREATY

If we can contain the powerful struggle of ideologies, and reduce it to manageable proportions, we can proceed with the transcendent task of disciplining the nuclear weapons which shadow our lives, and of finding a widened range of common enterprises between ourselves and those who live under communist rule. For, in the end, we live on one planet and we are part of one human family; and whatever the struggles that confront us, we must lose no chance to move forward towards a world of law and a world of disarmament.

*Address before the Canadian Parliament, Ottawa, May 17, 1961*


‡          ‡


Let us invoke the blessings of peace. And, as we build an international capacity to keep peace, let us join in dismantling the national capacity to wage war.

· · · · ·

. . . disarmament without checks is but a shadow and a community without law is but a shell.

*Address in New York City before the General
Assembly of the United Nations, September 25, 1961*

‡       ‡

Peace in space will help us naught once peace on earth is gone. World order will be secured only when the whole world has laid down these weapons which seem to offer us present security but threaten the future survival of the human race. That armistice day seems very far away. The vast resources of this planet are being devoted more and more to the means of destroying, instead of enriching, human life.

But the world was not meant to be a prison in which man awaits his execution. Nor has mankind survived the tests and the trials of thousands of years to surrender everything—including its existence—now. This Nation has the will and the faith to make a supreme effort to break the log jam on disarmament and nuclear tests—and we will persist until we prevail, until the rule of law has replaced the ever dangerous use of force.

*Annual Message to the Congress on the State of the
Union, January, 1962*

‡       ‡

A sea wall is not needed when the seas are calm. Sound disarmament agreements, deeply rooted in mankind's mutual interest in survival must serve as a bulwark against the tidal waves of war and its destructiveness.

・ ・ ・ ・ ・

. . . men now know that amassing of destructive power does not beget security; they know that polemics do not bring peace. Men's minds, men's hearts, and men's spiritual aspirations alike demand no less than a reversal of the course of recent history—a replacement of ever-growing stockpiles of destruction by ever-growing opportunities for human achievement.

*Letter to Secretary of State Dean Rusk on the opening of the Geneva Disarmament Conference, March 14, 1962*

‡            ‡

Beyond the drumfire of daily crisis, there is arising the outlines of a robust and vital world community, founded on nations secure in their own independence, and united by allegiance to world peace. It would be foolish to say that this world will be won tomorrow, or the day after. The processes of history are fitful and uncertain and aggravating. There will be frustrations and setbacks. There will be times of anxiety and gloom. The specter of thermonuclear war will continue to hang over mankind; and we must heed the advice of Oliver Wendell Holmes of "freedom leaning on her spear" until all nations are wise enough to disarm safely and effectively.

*University of California, Berkeley, March 23, 1962*

‡          ‡

. . . now, for the first time in many years, the path of peace may be open. No one can be certain what the future will bring. No one can say whether the time has come for an easing of the struggle. But history and our own conscience will judge us harsher if we do not now make every effort to test our hopes by action, and this is the place to begin. According to the ancient Chinese proverb, "A journey of a thousand miles must begin with a single step."

*Radio and television address to the American people on the Nuclear Test Ban Treaty, July 26, 1963*

‡          ‡

This Treaty is in our national interest. While experience teaches us to be cautious in our expectations and ever-vigilant in our preparations, there is no reason to oppose this hopeful step. It is rarely possible to recapture missed opportunities to achieve a more secure and peaceful world. To govern is to choose; and it is my judgment that the United States should move swiftly to make the most of the present opportunity and approve the pending Treaty.

*Message to the Senate on the Nuclear Test Ban Treaty,*
*August 8, 1963*

‡ ‡

This treaty will enable all of us who inhabit the earth, our children and children's children, to breathe easier, free from the fear of nuclear test fallout. It will curb the spread of nuclear weapons to other countries, thereby holding out hope for a more peaceful and stable world. It will slow down the nuclear arms race without impairing the adequacy of this Nation's arsenal or security, and it will offer a small but important foundation on which a world of law can be built.

*President's news conference, September 12, 1963,*
*stressing the importance of approval of the Nuclear*
*Test Ban Treaty by the United States Senate*

‡ ‡

Peace around the world, and progress here at home represent the hopes of all Americans. The United States Senate will vote on the treaty outlawing nuclear tests in the atmosphere. It is the first concrete limitation on the nuclear arms race since the bomb was invented. It enables all men and women, East and West, free and slave, now and in the future, to be free from radioactive fallout. It affords us all a small sign of hope that war can be averted; that the terrible destructive power of nuclear weapons can be abolished before they abolish us; that our children can inhabit a world in which freedom is secure, and the air is pure.

*Radio and television address to the Nation on the Nuclear Test Ban Treaty and the Tax Reduction Bill, September 18, 1963*

. . . . .

‡    ‡

Two years ago I told this body that the United States had proposed, and was willing to sign, a limited test ban treaty. Today that treaty has been signed. It will not put an end to war. It will not secure freedom for all. But it can be a lever, and Archimedes, in explaining the principles of the lever, was said to have declared to his friends: "Give me a place where I can stand—and I shall move the world."

. . . . .

Today we may have reached a pause in the cold war—but that is not a lasting peace. A test ban treaty is a milestone—but it is not the millennium. We have not been released from our obligations—we have been given an opportunity. And if we fail to make the most of this moment and this momentum—if we convert our newfound hopes and understandings into new walls and weapons of hostility—if this pause in the cold war merely leads to its renewal and not to its end—then the indictment of posterity will rightly point its finger at us all. But if we can stretch this pause into a period of cooperation—if both sides can now gain new confidence and experience in concrete collaborations for peace—if we can now be as bold and farsighted in the control of deadly weapons as we have been in their creation—then surely this first small step can be the start of a long and fruitful journey.

· · · · ·

. . . let us move up the steep and difficult path toward comprehensive disarmament, securing mutual confidence through mutual verification, and building the institutions of peace as we dismantle the engines of war. We must not let failure to agree on all points delay agreements where agreement is possible. And we must not put forward proposals for propaganda purposes.

*Address before the 18th General Assembly of the United Nations, September 20, 1963*

‡        ‡

In its first two decades the age of nuclear energy has been full of fear, yet never empty of hope. Today the fear is a little less and the hope a little greater. For the first time we have been able to reach an agreement which can limit the dangers of this age.

The agreement itself is limited, but its message of hope has been heard and understood not only by the peoples of the three originating nations, but by the peoples and governments of the hundred other countries that have signed. This treaty is the first fruit of labor in which multitudes have shared—citizens, legislators, statesmen, diplomats, and soldiers, too.

．．．．．

What the future will bring, no one of us can know. This first fruit of hope may or may not be followed by larger harvests. Even this limited treaty, great as it is with promise, can survive only if it has from others the determined support in letter and in spirit which I hereby pledge in behalf of the United States.

*On signing the Nuclear Test Ban Treaty,*
*October 7, 1963*

‡　　　　‡

# WESTERN UNITY AND THE
# COMPETITION WITH
# COMMUNISM

. . . civility is not a sign of weakness, and sincerity is always subject to proof. Let us never negotiate out of fear. But let us never fear to negotiate.

*Inaugural Address, January 20, 1961*

‡          ‡

The years ahead will demand of us all courage, sacrifice and the will to seize every opportunity to secure and to advance human liberty. In cooperation with one another, and all those around the globe who believe in the freedom of man, we can and we will succeed.

*Message to the Secretary General of NATO on the 12th anniversary of the signing of the North Atlantic Treaty, April 3, 1961*

‡          ‡

We intend to have a wider choice than humiliation or all-out nuclear action. We are willing to consider any arrangement or treaty in Germany consistent with the maintenance of peace and freedom. . . . We recognize the Soviet Union's historical concern about their security in Central and Eastern Europe, after a series of ravaging invasions. And we believe arrangements can be worked out to meet those concerns. The freedom of that city is not negotiable. We cannot negotiate with those who say, "What's mine is mine and what's yours is negotiable."

*Radio and television speech to the American people on the Berlin crisis, July 25, 1961*

‡        ‡

Fear is the oldest weapon in history. Throughout the life of mankind, it has been the resort, of those who could not hope to prevail by reason and persuasion. It will be repelled today, as it has been repelled in the past—not only by the steadfastness of free men but by the power of the arms which men will use to defend their freedom.

*On the occasion of the explosion by the USSR of a fifty-megaton bomb, October 30, 1961*

‡        ‡

Those who preach the doctrine of the inevitability of the class struggle and of the Communist success, should realize that in the last few years the great effort which has been made to unify economically the countries of the Free World, offers far greater promise than the sterile and broken promises of the Communist system. Against the Communist system of iron discipline, the Atlantic partnership will present a world of free choice. Against their predictions of our collapse, it will present a challenge of free nations working in harmony, and it will provide economically an effective answer to those boasts of their ultimately overtaking us.

*Address in New Orleans at the opening of the new Dockside Terminal, May 4, 1962*


‡        ‡


Progress is not only essential for the future of our people at home. It is also essential for our position in international affairs. Progress is the source of purpose and it is the source of power; and purpose and power are the weapons with which we oppose communism and fight for peace and justice in the world.

. . . . .

A stagnant nation, a torpid nation, a conservative nation, a nation committed to the past—such a nation could not hope to rally the people of the world against communism. Only a strong nation, an active nation, a nation moving always ahead, a nation dedicated to the future can lead the peoples of a revived Europe and an emergent Asia and Africa and Latin America. Armed by purpose and power we need have no fear about our capacity to deal with communism.

*There was a heavy rain at the Wheeling Stadium, Wheeling, West Virginia, September 27, 1962, and it became necessary for the President to cut short his remarks. The above is from the prepared text*

‡        ‡

A vital expanding economy in the free world is a strong counter to the threat of the world Communist movement.

*Upon signing the Trade Expansion Act of October 11, 1962*

‡        ‡

. . . at this point in history we can look back to many successes in the struggle to preserve freedom. Our nation is still daily winning unseen victories in the fight against communist subversion in the slums and hamlets, in the hospitals and schools, and in the offices of governments across a world bent on lifting itself. Two centuries of pioneering and growth must be telescoped into decades and even years. This is a field of action for which our history has prepared us, to which our aspirations have drawn us, and into which our national interest moves us.

*Special message to the Congress on free world defense and assistance programs, April 2, 1963*

‡          ‡

I have crossed the Atlantic, some 3,500 miles, at a crucial time in the life of the Grand Alliance. Our unity was forged in a time of danger; it must be maintained in a time of peace. Our Alliance was founded to deter a new war; it must now find the way to a new peace. Our strategy was born in a divided Europe, but it must look to the goal of European unity and an end to the divisions of people and countries. Our Alliance is in a period of transition, and that is as it should be. Western Europe is no longer weakened by conflict, but is fast becoming a full partner in prosperity and security. Western Europe is no longer the seedbed of world war, but an instrument of unity and an example of reconciliation. And Western Europe, finally, is no longer an area of assistance, but can now be a source of strength, to all the forces of freedom all around the globe.

*Remarks upon arriving in Germany, June 23, 1963*

‡     ‡

The problems of the Western world are, in many ways, different than they were 2,000 years ago, but our obligations as citizens remain the same—to defend our common heritage from those who would divide and destroy it; to develop and enrich that heritage so that it is passed on to those who come after us.

*On signing the Golden Book at the Rathaus in Cologne, June 23, 1963*

‡     ‡

Dante once said that the hottest places in hell are reserved for those who in a period of moral crisis maintain their neutrality.

*From a speech in Bonn, at the time of the signing of the charter establishing the German Peace Corps, June 24, 1963*

‡     ‡

. . . we are called to a great new mission. It is not a mission of self-defense alone—for that is a means, not an end. It is not a mission of arbitrary power—for we reject the idea of one nation dominating another. The mission is to create a new social order, founded on liberty and justice, in which men are the masters of their fate, in which states are the servants of their citizens, and in which all men and women can share a better life for themselves and their children.

*Frankfurt, Germany, June 25, 1963*

‡          ‡

I do believe in the necessity of great powers working together to preserve the human race, or otherwise we can be destroyed. This process can only be helped by the growing unity of the West, and we must all work towards that unity, for in unity there is strength . . . and any division or weakness only makes our task more difficult.

*Address before students at the Free University of Berlin, June 26, 1963*

‡          ‡

The contest will continue—the contest between those who see a monolithic world and those who believe in diversity—but it should be a contest in leadership and responsibility instead of destruction, a contest in achievement instead of intimidation. Speaking for the United States of America, I welcome such a contest. For we believe that truth is stronger than error—and that freedom is more enduring than coercion. And in the contest for a better life, all the world can be a winner.

*Address before the 18th Assembly of the United Nations, September 20, 1963*

‡ ‡

In short, when we think of peace in this country, let us think both of our capacity to deter aggression and our goal of true disarmament. Let us think of both the strength of our western alliances and the areas of East-West cooperation.

*University of Maine, October 19, 1963*

‡ ‡

# LATIN AMERICA

Let all our neighbors know that we shall join with them to oppose aggression or subversion anywhere in the Americas. And let every other power know that this hemisphere intends to remain the master of its own house.

*Inaugural Address, January 20, 1961*

‡          ‡

Let us once again transform the American continent into a vast crucible of revolutionary ideas and efforts—a tribute to the power of the creative energies of free men and women—an example to all the world that liberty and progress walk hand in hand. Let us once again awaken our American revolution until it guides the struggle of people everywhere—not with an imperialism of force or fear—but the rule of courage and freedom and hope for the future of man.

. . . . .

The revolutions which gave us birth ignited, in the words of Thomas Paine, "a spark never to be extinguished." And across vast, turbulent continents these American ideals still stir man's struggle for national independence and individual freedom. But as we welcome the spread of the American revolution to other lands, we must also remember that our own struggle . . . is not yet finished. Our hemisphere's mission is not yet completed. For our unfulfilled task is to demonstrate to the entire world that man's unsatisfied aspiration for economic progress and social justice can best be achieved by free men working within a framework of democratic institutions. If we can do this in our own hemisphere, and for our own people, we may yet realize the prophecy of the great Mexican patriot, Benito Juárez, that "democracy is the destiny of future humanity."

*White House reception for members of the Congress and the Diplomatic Corps of the Latin American republics, March 13, 1961*

‡ ‡

The tasks before us are vast, the problems difficult, the challenges unparalleled. But we carry with us the vision of a new and better world, and the unlimited power of free men guided by free governments. And I believe that our ultimate success will make us proud to have lived and worked at this historic moment in the life of our hemisphere.

*Message to the Inter-American Economic and Social
Conference at Punta del Este, Uruguay,
August 5, 1961*

‡ ‡

I can offer no better advice than that given by José Martí to his fellow exiles in 1895 when the hour of Cuban independence was at hand. "Let the tenor of our words be," Martí said, "especially in public matters, not the useless clamor of fear's vengeance which does not enter our hearts, but the honest weariness of an oppressed people who hope through their emancipation from a government convicted of uselessness and malevolence for a government of their own, which is capable and worthy." "Let them see in us," Martí said, "constructive Americans and not empty bitterness."

*Remarks made in Miami at the presentation of the
flag of the Cuban Invasion Brigade,
December 29, 1962*

‡ ‡

One of the things which I have taken the greatest interest in has been attempting to pursue an example which was long neglected. And that was the one set by President Franklin Roosevelt to emphasize that the United States is not only good neighbors, which we were in the thirties, but also friends and associates in a great effort to build in this hemisphere an Alliance for Progress, an effort to prove that in this hemisphere, from top to bottom, in all of the countries whether they be Latin or North American, that there is a common commitment to freedom, to equality of opportunity, to a chance for all to prove that prosperity can be the handmaiden of freedom, and to show to the world a very bright star here in this country and indeed, in the entire hemisphere.

*Remarks to the League of United Latin American Citizens, in Houston, November 21, 1963*

‡      ‡

# Part III

# THE FREE SOCIETY

All of our early revolutionary leaders I think echoed the words of Thomas Jefferson that "the disease of liberty is catching." And some of you may remember the exchange between Benjamin Franklin and Thomas Paine. Benjamin Franklin said, "Where freedom lives, there is my home." And Thomas Paine said, "Where freedom is not, there is my home." I think all of us who believe in freedom feel a sense of community with all those who are free, but I think we also feel an even stronger sense of community with those who are not free but who some day will be free.

*Reception marking African Freedom Day,*
*April 15, 1961*

‡          ‡

. . . freedom is not merely a word or an abstract theory, but the most effective instrument for advancing the welfare of man. We face new conditions and we must devise new remedies to meet them, and we are confident that we will move forward.

· · · · ·

We live in a hemisphere whose own revolution has given birth to the most powerful forces of the modern age—the search for the freedom and self-fulfillment of man. We meet to carry on that revolution to shape the future as we have the past.

*Message to the Inter-American Economic and Social Conference at Punta del Este, Uruguay, August 5, 1961*

‡      ‡

For a city or a people to be truly free, they must have the secure right, without economic, political or police pressure, to make their own choice and to live their own lives.

*Address in New York City before the General Assembly of the United Nations, September 25, 1961*

‡      ‡

It is well to love liberty, for it demands much of those who live by it. Liberty is not content to share mankind.

*St. Patrick's Day speech, March 17, 1962*

✠         ✠

What freedom alone can bring is the liberation of the human mind and spirit which finds its greatest flowering in the free society.

*Speech in behalf of the National Cultural Center, November 29, 1962*

✠         ✠

. . . a free society places greater burdens upon every citizen than any other kind of system. It requires an ability to make a choice, to have those qualities of judgment and self-restraint which permit a democracy to operate.

*Fiftieth anniversary luncheon of the Delta Sigma Theta Sorority, January 12, 1963*

✠         ✠

Almost two centuries have passed since a small, weak nation, a beachhead on a continent, began the great experiment of democracy in a world where government by the consent of the governed was extinguished for 2,000 years. As Jefferson prophesied, there have been many years of desolation and destruction. It seems to me that it is our responsibility in this year of change and hope to prove that we are equal to this great inheritance, to make it possible for the four freedoms which Franklin Roosevelt so eloquently described in another time of peril and danger 20 years ago—to make sure that those four freedoms, indeed the great concept of indivisible freedom is made available to all of our people, to all of our citizens, and to bear our part of the burden as we have for so many years in making that great concept available to all people.

*Speech at the 50th annual meeting of the Anti-Defamation League of B'nai B'rith, January 31, 1963*

‡                    ‡

. . . unless liberty flourishes in all lands, it cannot flourish in one. Conceived in one hall, it must be carried out in many. Thus, the seeds of the American Revolution had been brought earlier from Europe, and they later took root around the world.

*Address at the Assembly Hall at the Paulskirche in Frankfurt, June 25, 1963*

If our nations can set an example of vigorous freedom in action, if we can achieve full employment, control inflation, reduce inequalities, and spread the blessings of prosperity to all of our people, if we can fulfill each family's need, not only for a full day's work at a fair day's wages, but for schools and hospitals and housing and other services—then we can more surely and strongly sustain our commitments to Western security, lay the foundation for a democratic Atlantic Community, and inspire freedom and hope in other lands. Together let us build sturdy mansions of freedom, mansions that all the world can admire and copy but that no tyrant can ever enter. It will not be easy. It is not easy to secure progress through democracy, but in my opinion it is the only way that progress can be assured.

*Dinner given in President Kennedy's honor by President Segni of Italy, July 1, 1963*

‡　　　　‡

# THE DEFENSE OF FREEDOM

We observe today not a victory of party but a celebration of freedom—symbolizing an end as well as a beginning—signifying renewal as well as change.

. . . . .

In the long history of the world, only a few generations have been granted the role of defending freedom in its hour of maximum danger. I do not shrink from this responsibility, I welcome it.

*Inaugural Address, January 20, 1961*

‡        ‡

If the self-discipline of the free cannot match the iron discipline of the mailed fist—in economic, political, scientific and all the other kinds of struggles as well as the military—then the peril to freedom will continue to rise.

*Address before the American Society of Newspaper Editors, April 20, 1961*

‡        ‡

. . . the cause of human freedom has been threatened on many occasions since the system of free choice and democracy was developed in sunlit Greece more than twenty-four hundred years ago. And yet from each threat and indeed from each defeat, as well as from each success, it has ultimately emerged unconquered.

That is why in the face of an ominous future we can share that faith which Winston Churchill expressed more than a half-century ago. "Humanity will not be cast down."

We are going along, along the same high road, and already behind the distant mountains the sun can be seen —and will be seen again.

*Address to the 39th annual convention of the National Association of Broadcasters, May 8, 1961*

‡        ‡

. . . while we believe not only in the force of arms but in the force of right and reason, we have learned that reason does not always appeal to unreasonable men—that it is not always true that "a soft answer turneth away wrath"—and that right does not always make might.

·  ·  ·  ·  ·

. . . while we shall negotiate freely, we shall not negotiate freedom. Our answer to the classic question of Patrick Henry is still no—life is not so dear, and peace is not so precious, "as to be purchased at the price of chains and slavery." . . . "We will always seek peace—but we will never surrender."

*University of Washington, on its 100th anniversary, November 16, 1961*

‡                    ‡

. . . on the strength of our free economy rests the hope of all free nations. We shall not fail that hope, for free men and free nations must prosper and they must prevail.

*From an address and question-and-answer period at the Economic Club of New York, December 14, 1962*

‡                    ‡

. . . your small brigade is a tangible reaffirmation that the human desire for freedom and independence is essentially unconquerable. Your conduct and valor are proof that although Castro and his fellow dictators may rule nations, they do not rule people; that they may imprison bodies, but they do not imprison spirits; that they may destroy the exercise of liberty, but they cannot eliminate the determination to be free. And by helping to free you, the United States has been given the opportunity to demonstrate once again that all men who fight for freedom are our brothers, and shall be until your country and others are free.

*Upon the presentation of the flag of the Cuban Invasion Brigade, December 29, 1962*

‡ ‡

Let me ask you to lift your eyes beyond the dangers of today, to the hopes of tomorrow, beyond the freedom merely of this city of Berlin, or your country of Germany, to the advance of freedom everywhere, beyond the wall to the day of peace with justice, beyond yourselves and ourselves to all mankind.

. . . . .

Freedom is indivisible, and when one man is enslaved all are not free. When all are free, then we can look forward to that day when this city will be joined as one and this country and this great Continent of Europe in a peaceful and hopeful globe.

*Speech made in the Rudolph Wilde Platz, Berlin, June 26, 1963*

‡ ‡

We cannot fulfill our vision and our commitment and our interest in a free and diverse future without unceasing vigilance, devotion, and most of all, perseverance, a willingness to stay with it, a willingness to do with fatigue, a willingness not to accept easy answers, but instead, to maintain the burden, as the people of this State have done for 100 years, and as the United States must do the rest of this century until finally we live in a peaceful world.

Therefore, I think this country will continue its commitments to support the world of freedom, for as we discharge that commitment we are heeding the command which Brigham Young heard from the Lord more than a century ago, the command he conveyed to his followers, "Go as pioneers . . . to a land of peace."

*Address in Salt Lake City at the Mormon Tabernacle, September 26, 1963*

‡      ‡

John Boyle O'Reilly who came to Boston by way of a penal colony in Western Australia, wrote, "Freedom is more than a resolution—he is not free who is free alone."

To those who in our time have lost their freedom, or who through the ages have never won it, there is a converse to this message. No one—in the darkest cell, the remotest prison, under the most unyielding tyranny—is ever entirely lost in bondage while there are yet free men in the world. As this be our faith let it also be our pride.

*St. Patrick's Day speech, March 17, 1962*

‡      ‡

# THE VICTORY OF MAN

In setting the goal of our society at the realization of human dignity, we reach for the highest of stars and seek the outer limits of human capability. In this, now as always the new world for the spirit, the labor of free men is both the reward and the way.

*Labor Day, 1961*

‡　　　　‡

There is . . . the knowledge that suffering must make both a people and a man more certain of the right, while triumph brings with it the command to respect that right.

*Excerpt from a statement on the Jewish High Holy Days, September 6, 1961*

‡　　　　‡

What more can be said today, regarding all the dark and tangled problems we face than : Let there be light.

*University of Washington, on its 100th anniversary, November 16, 1961*

‡          ‡

. . . it is not our military might, or our higher standard of living, that has most distinguished us from our adversaries. It is our belief that the state is the servant of the citizen and not his master.

This basic clash of ideas and wills is but one of the forces reshaping our globe—swept as it is by the tides of hope and fear, by crises in the headlines today that become mere footnotes tomorrow. . . . For every apparent blessing contains the seeds of danger—every area of trouble gives out a ray of hope—and the one unchangeable certainty is that nothing is certain or unchangeable.

· · · · ·

This is our guide for the present and our vision for the future—a free community of nations, independent but interdependent, uniting north and south, east and west, in one great family of man, outgrowing and transcending the hates and fears that rend our age.

*Annual Message to the Congress on the State of the Union, January, 1962*

We welcome the views of others. We seek a free flow of information across national boundaries and oceans, across iron curtains and stone walls. We are not afraid to entrust the American people with unpleasant facts, foreign ideas, alien philosophies, and competitive values. For a nation that is afraid to let its people judge the truth and falsehood in an open market is a nation that is afraid of its people.

*On the 20th anniversary of the Voice of America, February 26, 1962*

‡　　　‡

As every past generation has had to disenthrall itself from an inheritance of truisms and stereotypes, so in our own time we must move on from the reassuring repetition of stale phrases to a new, difficult, but essential confrontation with reality.

For the great enemy of the truth is very often not the lie—deliberate, contrived, and dishonest—but the myth—persistent, persuasive, and unrealistic. Too often we hold fast to the clichés of our forebears. We subject all facts to a prefabricated set of interpretations. We enjoy the comfort of opinion without the discomfort of thought.

*Commencement address at Yale University, June 11, 1962*

‡          ‡

There is an old saying that only in the winter can you tell which trees are evergreens.

*To a group of student volunteers participating in Operation Crossroads Africa, June 22, 1962*

‡          ‡

Much has been given to us, and much is therefore expected from us.

*Labor Day, September 3, 1962*

‡          ‡

. . . we seek not the worldwide victory of one nation or system but a worldwide victory of man. The modern globe is too small, its weapons are too destructive, and its disorders are too contagious to permit any other kind of victory.

. . . . .

We are not lulled by the momentary calm of the sea or the somewhat clearer skies above. We know the turbulence that lies below, and the storms that are beyond the horizon this year. But now the winds of change appear to be blowing more strongly than ever, in the world of communism as well as our own. For 175 years we have sailed with the tides of human freedom in our favor. We steer our ship with hope, as Thomas Jefferson said, "leaving Fear astern."

*Annual Message to the Congress, January 14, 1963*

‡        ‡

Peace has her victories as well as war, and this was one of the victories for the human spirit today.

*Radio and television address after the flight of Astronaut L. Gordon Cooper, May 16, 1963*

‡        ‡

. . . life is never easy. There is work to be done and obligations to be met—obligations to truth, to justice, and to liberty.

*University of Berlin, June 26, 1963*

‡ ‡

The problems of the world cannot possibly be solved by skeptics or cynics, whose horizons are limited by the obvious realities. We need men who can dream of things that never were, and ask why not. It matters not how small a nation is that seeks world peace and freedom, for, to paraphrase a citizen of my country, "the humblest nation of all the world, when clad in the armor of a righteous cause, is stronger than all the hosts of Error."

So we are all idealists. We are all visionaries. Let it not be said of this Atlantic generation that we left ideals and visions to the past, nor purpose and determination to our adversaries. We have come too far, we have sacrificed too much, to disdain the future now. And we shall ever remember what Goethe told us—that the "highest wisdom, the best that mankind ever knew" was the realization that "he only earns his freedom and existence who daily conquers them anew."

*Address before the Irish Parliament in Dublin, June 28, 1963*

‡ ‡

# RELIGION . . .

*During the campaign for the Presidential nomination,
Kennedy confronted the religious question directly. It
was understood that the voters of West Virginia were
afraid of Catholics. Kennedy appeared before them in
April and said:*

. . . so when any man stands on the steps of the Capitol and takes the oath of office of President, he is swearing to support the separation of church and state, he puts one hand on the Bible and raises the other hand to God as he takes the oath. And if he breaks his oath, he is not only committing a crime against the Constitution, for which the Congress can impeach him—and should impeach him—but he is committing a sin against God.

*Kennedy then raised his right hand and placed his left
hand on an imaginary Bible. He repeated softly, "A
sin against God, for he has sworn on the Bible."*

*During the political campaign, the subject of Catholicism weighed heavily on Kennedy's progress. He spoke
of it often, in speeches to Americans of all religions.
On one occasion he said:*

I am not a Catholic candidate for President. I am the Democratic Party's candidate for President who happens also to be a Catholic. I do not speak for my church on

public matters . . . and the Church does not speak
for me.

*Later, in another speech, Kennedy said:*

If I should lose on the real issues, I shall return to my
seat in the Senate, satisfied that I have tried my best and
was fairly judged. But if this election is decided on the
basis that forty million Americans lost their chance of
being President on the day they were baptized, then it is
the whole Nation that will be the loser.

‡          ‡

. . . man holds in his mortal hands the power to
abolish all forms of human poverty and forms of human
life. And yet the same revolutionary beliefs for which
our forebears fought are still at issue around the globe—
the belief that the rights of man come not from the generosity of the state but from the hand of God.

*Inaugural Address, January 20, 1961*

‡          ‡

In the words of a great President, whose birthday we honor today, closing his final State of the Union Message sixteen years ago, "We pray that we may be worthy of the unlimited opportunities that God has given us."

*State of the Union Message, January 30, 1961, in reference to Franklin D. Roosevelt's birthday*

‡          ‡

It is an ironic fact that in this nuclear age, when the horizon of human knowledge and human experience has passed far beyond any that any age has ever known, that we turn back at this time to the older source of wisdom and strength, to the words of the prophets and the saints, who tell us that faith is more powerful than doubt, that hope is more potent than despair, and that only through the love that is sometimes called charity can we conquer those forces within ourselves and throughout all the world that threaten the very existence of mankind.

. . . . .

Keeping in mind that "when a man's ways please the Lord, he maketh even his enemies to be at peace with him," let us go forth to lead this land that we love, joining in the prayer of General George Washington in 1783, "That God would have you in His holy protection, that He would incline the hearts of the citizens . . . to entertain a brotherly love and affection one for another . . . and finally that He would most graciously be pleased to dispose us all to do justice, to love mercy and to demean ourselves with . . . the characteristics of the Divine Author of our blessed religion, without an humble imitation of whose example we can never hope to be a happy nation."

. . . . .

Religious freedom has no significance unless it is accompanied by conviction.

. . . . .

We must recognize that human collaboration is not enough, that in times such as these we must reach beyond ourselves if we are to seek ultimate courage and infinite wisdom.

. . . . .

Every President has taken comfort and courage when told . . . that the Lord "will be with thee. He will not fail thee nor forsake thee. Fear not—neither be thou dismayed."

. . . . .

I do not regard religion as a weapon in the cold war. I regard it as the essence of the differences which separate those on the other side of the Iron Curtain and ourselves.

. . . . .

We cannot have religious freedom without political freedom, and therefore what we really need is not to confuse a system of freedom with one of disinterest, uninterest, cynicism, materialism.

*Dedication breakfast of International Christian Leadership, Inc., February 9, 1961*

. . . we take our lesson and our theme from the Bible and the story of Nehemias, which tells us that when the children of Israel returned from captivity they determined to rebuild the walls of Jerusalem, in spite of the threats of the enemy. The wall was built and the peace was preserved. But it was written, "Of them that built on the wall . . . with one of his hands he did the work, and with the other he held the sword."

We hold the sword, and we are determined to maintain our strength and our commitments. But we also hold in our hand the trowel. We are determined to build in our own country, so that those who come after us . . . will find available to them all of the great resources that we now have.

*Big Cedar, Oklahoma, on the opening of the Ouachita National Forest Road, October 29, 1961*

‡           ‡

It has always seemed to me that when we all—regardless of our particular religious convictions—draw our guidance and inspiration, and really in a sense moral direction from the same general area, the Bible, the Old and the New Testaments, we have every reason to believe that our various religious denominations should live together in the closest harmony.

*National Conference of Christians and Jews,*
*November 21, 1961*

‡          ‡

There is a quotation from Lincoln . . . He said, "I believe there is a God. I see the storm coming and I believe He has a hand in it. If He has a part and place for me, I believe that I am ready."

We see the storm coming, and we believe He has a hand in it, and if He has a place and a part for us, I believe we are ready.

*Tenth annual Presidential prayer breakfast,*
*March 1, 1962*

‡          ‡

. . . the Bible tells us that "there is a time for every purpose under the heaven . . . a time to cast away stones, and a time to gather stones together." . . . I believe it is time for us all to gather stones together to build this country as it must be built in the coming years.

*Speech before the United States Chamber of Commerce on its 50th anniversary, April 30, 1962*

‡        ‡

Many years ago, the great British explorer George Mallory, who was to die on Mount Everest, was asked why did he want to climb it. He said, "Because it is there."

Well space is there, and we're going to climb it, and the moon and the planets are there, and new hopes for knowledge and peace are there. And, therefore, as we set sail we ask God's blessing on the most hazardous and dangerous and greatest adventure on which man has ever embarked.

*Discussing the Nation's space effort at an address at Rice University, September 12, 1962*

‡        ‡

Christmas is truly the universal holiday of all men. It is the day when all of us dedicate our thoughts to others; when all are reminded that mercy and compassion are the enduring virtues; when all show, by small deeds and large and by acts, that it is more blessed to give than to receive.

. . . . .

Christmas is the day when we remind ourselves that man can and must live in peace with his neighbors and that it is the peacemakers who are truly blessed. In this year . . . we greet each other at Christmas with some special sense of the blessings of peace. This has been a year of peril when the peace has been sorely threatened. But it has been a year when peril was faced and when reason ruled. As a result, we may talk, at this Christmas, just a little bit more confidently of peace on earth, good will to men. As a result, the hopes of the American people are perhaps a little higher. We have much yet to do. We still need to ask that God bless everyone. But yet I think we can enter this season of good will with more than usual joy in our hearts.

*The Pageant of Peace Ceremonies,*
*December 17, 1962*

‡          ‡

We need the faith which has sustained and guided this Nation for one hundred seventy five long and short years. We are all builders of the future, and whether we build as public servants or private citizens, whether we build at the national or the local level, whether we build in foreign or domestic affairs, we know the truth of the ancient Psalm, "Except the Lord build the house, they labour in vain that build it."

This morning we pray together; this evening apart. But each morning and each evening, let us remember the advice of my fellow Bostonian, the Reverend Phillips Brooks: "Do not pray for easy lives. Pray to be stronger men! Do not pray for tasks equal to your powers. Pray for powers equal to your tasks."

*Eleventh annual Presidential prayer breakfast,
February 7, 1963*

‡        ‡

As our power has grown, so has our peril. Today we give our thanks, most of all, for the ideals of honor and faith we inherit from our forefathers—for the decency of purpose, steadfastness of resolve and strength of will, for the courage and the humility, which they possessed and which we must seek every day to emulate. As we express our gratitude, we must never forget that the highest appreciation is not to utter words but to live by them.

Let us therefore proclaim our gratitude to Providence for manifold blessings—let us be humbly thankful for inherited ideals—and let us resolve to share those blessings and those ideals with our fellow human beings throughout the world.

*Thanksgiving Day Proclamation, November 5, 1963*

"Your old men shall dream dreams, your young men shall see visions," the Bible tells us, and "where there is no vision, the people perish."

*A dinner honoring Representative Albert Thomas, November 21, 1963, at the Coliseum in Houston*

‡            ‡

We in this country, in this generation, are—by destiny rather than choice—the watchmen on the walls of world freedom. We ask, therefore, that we may be worthy of our power and responsibility, that we may exercise our strength with wisdom and restraint, and that we may achieve in our time and for all time the ancient vision of "peace on earth, good will toward men." That must always be our goal, and the righteousness of our cause must always underlie our strength. For as was written long ago: "except the Lord keep the city, the watchman waketh but in vain."

*Speech prepared for delivery at the Trade Mart in Dallas, November 22, 1963. The President was assassinated before the speech could be given*

‡            ‡